Chakras For Beginners:

The Ultimate Guide on How to Balance Chakras, Improve Spiritual and Emotional Health, Strengthen Aura, Chakras Meditation Practice

By

Brittany Samons

Table of Contents

Introduction 5

Chapter 1. History Of Chakra Philosophy 7

Chapter 2. Chakras and Their Functions 9

Chapter 3. Chakra Balancing 19

Chapter 4. Meditation Examples For 7 Major Chakras ... 29

Conclusion 34

Thank You Page 35

Chakras For Beginners: The Ultimate Guide on How to Balance Chakras, Improve Spiritual and Emotional Health, Strengthen Aura, Chakras Meditation Practice

By Brittany Samons

© Copyright 2015 Brittany Samons

Reproduction or translation of any part of this work beyond that permitted by section 107 or 108 of the 1976 United States Copyright Act without permission of the copyright owner is unlawful. Requests for permission or further information should be addressed to the author.

This publication is designed to provide accurate and authoritative information in regard to the subject matter covered. This work is sold with the understanding that the publisher is not engaged in rendering legal, accounting, or other professional services. If legal advice or other expert assistance is required, the services of a competent professional person should be sought.

First Published, 2015

Printed in the United States of America

Introduction

Chakras are energy helms of light that actually receive, accomplish, regulate and emit energy. They always attach the emotional, physical and divine energy within you to the divine and higher-dimensional loveliness around you.

From the view of spiritual and healing development, each chakra is a sole and a perfect reflection of physical, mental, emotional and spiritual health. Like discrete and multifaceted computer disks, chakras include a wealth of individual information revealing how you feel, experience, narrate, express and cooperate with yourself, others and also the world around you.

There are several chakras within the mortal energy field and each and every one has an individual persistence and purpose. Among all of them, seven chakras are really very important, because these primary chakras directly relate to your 7 primary chakras, unswervingly relate to action, movement and energy or power exchanges. There are actually higher or advanced chakra centers where they connect you with extended levels of awareness and multidimensional powers and energies along with feet and hand centers which are known as secondary chakras.

Chapter 1. History Of Chakra Philosophy

Chakra concept from eastern comes from Indian culture, exactly from Hindu philosophy. The word Chakra is Hindi in origin and describes "spinning wheel". Now chakra's system is now frequently used in the West healing and spiritual practices. It has become very popular not least because of its openness for both color healing applications and meditation. They are also at the origin of the human atmosphere, a magnetic and attractive field that stands outside the discernable body. The aura is completely visible through professional (Kirlian) photography device and to persons who have the skill or ability of being able to see the aura with his/her own eyes. Some of the curative color applications that have arisen from our modern empathetic of the aura contain aura-soma, where bottles of colored fluids are used to assist diagnose states and start healing in the patient.

Again, chakra balancing is a complete system of individual healing, though, and can be done without the help of a therapist. Chakra balancing is considered as a rebalancing of powers and energies at all levels, having emotional, physical and psychic. The chakras all together form an energy or power system, relating exactly to a number of points or areas in the body.

Through these area's color is capable of entering and is reflected and the state and the advent of such color eminences may alter according to our emotional, mental and physical states. It assists us to know and realize how chakras do their work if we recall that this is an all-inclusive system. On the other hand, we can also say that if we are looking at healing and curing the heart chakra, we must have to be thinking healing not only from the corner of our mental and physical condition but also concerning our emotional happiness, since both sites relate to the roles of the heart.

Chapter 2. Chakras and Their Functions

Chakras or rotating energy centers are extremely important part here. Just as the visible body has dynamic and slight organs, the energy body has main, slight and mini chakras. Main Chakras are actually energy centers, which generally are about 3 to 4 inches in diameter. They switch and invigorate the major and vigorous organs of the visible physical body. They exactly look like power stations that provide life energy or prone to various organs. When the power stations have any breakdown, the consistent vital organs become very sick or diseased because they do not have sufficient life energy to function or work properly!

The chakras have some important functions and purposes:

1. They engross, digest and allocate prana to the various parts of the physical body.

2. The Chakras rheostat and invigorate, and are liable for the proper working of the whole body and its different organs and areas. The endocrine glands in the human body are fully controlled and energized by

certain of the main chakras. These glands can be enthused or reserved by operating or controlling the main chakras. A lot of illnesses are caused partially by the broken of the chakras.

3. Again, it can be noticed that some chakras are centers of psychic abilities. Beginning of certain chakras may consequence in the growth of convincing psychic faculties. For instance, among the calmest and harmless chakras to trigger are the hand minor chakras. These chakras are located at the midpoint of the palms. By triggering these chakras, one develops the skill to feel delicate energies and the capacity to feel and sense various parts of the aura.

What Do Chakras Teach Us?

The chakras clarify us about each level of our humanoid experience from the ordinary to the inspirational, and from the embryonic to the devout. The lessons and teachings of the chakras anthropomorphize every facet of our life. It can best define how we as energy bodies use our energy.

Here each chakra is "fully connected" with an endocrine gland and different organs and body constructions. Everything in your corporeal body and its terminologies like thinking, talking, loving, etc. need some procedure of energy.

The 7 Chakras

The most vital 7 Chakras are the main energy centers in our physical body in which energy streams through. Congested energy in our major 7 Chakras can often guide to illness so it's significant to realize what each Chakra indicates and what we can fix to possess this energy flowing easily.

Root Chakra

Its color is completely red and it is positioned at the perineum, the base of your back. It is the Chakra contiguous to the earth. Its purpose and role is concerned with possible grounding and bodily existence. This Chakra is related to your legs, bones, feet, large intestine and adrenal glands. It reins your fight or flight reply. Obstruction may manifest as fear, procrastination, fear and defensiveness

Sexual or Sacral Chakra

This sacral chakra's color is orange and it is situated between your navel and the base of your spine. It is related to your lower abdomen, circulatory system, kidneys, bladder and your generative organs and glands. It is careful with emotion. This chakra indicates desire, pleasure, sexuality, procreation and creativity. Obstruction may manifest as emotional problems, obsessive behavior and sexual blame

Brow or Third Eye Chakra

The teachings of the 6th chakra can be problematic to master, but once you fix, you will never set the world the same. This energy handles with deciphering between all the trained traditions, customs, beliefs and coming up with your personal fact. Society does not explain you how to accelerate this chakra. Actually, the "matrix" does all to keep you stuck in a delusion.

The purpose this chakra is one of the more stimulating and inspiring lessons are because sometimes it's cooler to live in a delusion than to face the fact and make your moves consequential. For instance, have you ever acknowledged someone who was with a friend that was cheating on all of them? Everyone discerned about it, but the individual who was being embittered on. He or she might have had a gut feeling that their mate is not being truthful but somewhat live in an illusion that altogether is fine as oppose to facing the truth and perhaps separating from that one.

In addition to the main example of discriminating between truth and delusion, the brow chakra handles your intellect, ability to learn, impartial reasoning, insight, and wisdom and mind power. Here, mind power is another sample of the energy-meaning arguments related to these chakras.

Impartial reasoning is when you can contact something without prejudice. Think of how a magistrate would be in their law court. When hearing from the plan tiff and defendant, a magistrate should not let biases, preconceived notions and rumor command to their result. The flow of this brow energy includes finding the final truth after due assiduousness. This needs you to "take yourself out" of the image and measure it from a godlike opinion.

Heart Chakra

Hate and love are two very important terms in human life. They are some of the sturdiest energies. They are both our two ends of the similar frequency. One can easily make you seal all warm and uncertain inside while the other one can keep you away from that touch of paradise.

The heart chakra is curving with full of energy when you adore yourself, nature and others without situations and restrictions. On the other hand, the opposite of this love is resentment, betrayal, jealousy, and hatred. No one can make you hate or love them, this emotion is self-generated. Love is completely natural, but family, society, media and such describe us to dislike or hate. Typically, when someone has full of hate for others, it's an outcome of peripheral forces fixing seeds in their heads.

Total love and forgiveness is energetic for your heart liveliness. Jealousy, rage and anger are harmful to this countless energy. A lot can be completed out of one's movements from a result of egotism and love for his or her associated energy beings. The heart chakra perfectly lies at the midpoint of the 7 energy points and helps as the "gateway" to our advanced self.

Solar Plexus Chakra

We all know that the sun is yellow and gives solar energy, so the solar plexus chakra associates to your individual power. Individual power can appear in the form of pride, a sense of identity, self-confidence and will and strength. Everyone is possibly familiar with the words "willpower". Power explains energy so determined is the energy it takes to keep moving forward.

It is known that the solar plexus chakra is directly related to the stomach. It also handles the processing or absorption of information. This could stretch, rise to instinctive feelings. Instinctive feelings typically derive from, your valuation of a condition and you just develop a feeling in your intuitive be it ok or not.

When you deeply study about the chakras, you realize that your emotional energy stays in solar plexus part. The feeling of fear has been identified to make people feel sick to their stomach. Again, fear, possibly the worst emotion you have, is minor chakra energy.

Crown Chakra

This is the highest self. True nature is an active divine being with a soul that is everlasting. The crown chakra is actually your linking to the Source of all.

This crown chakra is the fact of intuition. This is more than an instinctive feeling because this is not based on your assessments and observations. This instinct comes from a heavenly source or a source that is not associated with the physical. Here our true nature is completely spirit. Spirit is the representation and power of the soul. Now everybody must have a question of soul. What is it? The soul is what lives for eternity and the life is its appearance.

We are connected and surrounded by the energy of the crown chakra. Our powers and energies are linked with each other. The lengthier you are with somebody and the sturdier energetic linking you have, the more you will recognize their behavior, about to fix and touch. Think about the linking a mother has with her children. There's no false that a mother has what is recognized as "mother's perception". We all came from a mother that resides in her solar plexus part, and was birthed through her holy canal or sacral chakra. This power is a bond that is so robust and it cannot be broken by being separate physically.

Your mental awareness lies in this very important crown chakra. Cognitive abilities are not corporeal so it is of mystical nature. Psychic contains "sighted into the future" and forecasting events in such, but mental awareness means just recognizing something that is outside the five senses. With the appearance of scientific information and entree to esoteric and occult knowledge by way of the books and internet, we now have a healthier understanding of our mystical nature.

Throat Chakra

The fifth seal, which is also known as throat chakra is one of categorical love expressed. This level is associated with sound, voice, expressing ourselves visibly and stating our meanings out into the world for better development of the world. It is about speaking truth. Its place is the neck and is associated with the element of air or interplanetary. It links with the process of display: first, we have a belief (in the sixth plane); if we want to carry this stimulus into form, at some topic we must, most possible, express this idea so that it can carry its way down the closures in the thickest form of matter and appearance on the first plane. This stage of development is frequently seen as a grandmother or grandfather who has an absolute love for her grandchild and is gifted to freely, effortlessly and openly direct that love.

Chapter 3. Chakra Balancing

Importance of Chakra Balancing

Keeping our physical body animated, healthy and active well is a complex exercise in complementary. It's known as homeostasis, and it preserves all the hormones, substances, and processes of the body in agreement with each other. If body deviates from a state of homeostasis, we're in big trouble.

In the same technique, our chakras must be in symmetry and allied with each other.

When chakras are out of balance, it can have a deep impact on mental, physical, emotional and spiritual health. When they are totally out of alignment, both our lives and bodies are likely to be improper balance as well. You may hook that you are illness- or disaster-prone, or that your lives are confused, unhappy or unsatisfying.

How to Express if You Need Chakra Balancing?

It is possible to express energetically. Energy flows through the chakra system generally in two ways. The first one is, it flows or circulates up and down in central channel, base of spine to upper of head, fixing the chakras. Second, it does not flow vertically; it only flows horizontally, in an interchange of energy with the cosmos.

A balanced chakra system:

1) When energy flows spontaneously vertically, reaching all the chakras: no one of the chakras is blocked. On the other hand, energy flows spontaneously horizontally: each chakra interchanges energy easily with the cosmos.

2) Nor any of the chakras is significantly more open or spiraling faster or slower than the others: no one is substantively feverish or underactive in comparison to all the others.

3) Besides, every chakra is opened to the degree required to support your health and spiritual improvement: no one of the seven chakras is being open too wide, or closed down too close-fitting.

4) Neither the higher chakras nor the minor chakras are over-emphasized.

Methods For Chakra Balancing

Chakra balancing, in concert with other methods, often delivers a great deal of emotional healing as well as spiritual healing and can aid prevent physical illness, too. Many of those energy healers will spend a substantial quantity of their time with you curing the chakras such as opening, balancing, aligning as well as energizing them. A proficient energy remedial can be decent not only for maintaining the chakras, but also to become a feel for your individual chakras.

However, there are also a lot of methods that you physically can use for chakra balancing and maintaining. Remember that the way to get ready any energy-work technique effective is to do it attentively, with the sacred goal to heal. Besides, it's the intention rather than the genuine technique that's import.

Meditation With Crystals

It denotes the color of a definite chakra is thought to make stronger and balance that chakra. For illustration, the Throat Chakra relates to the color blue. Blue crystals just like blue lace agate are supposed to aid balance communication and fetch harmony to the Throat Chakra.

Working With A Singing Bowl

Tibetan singing bowls are usually made of brass. When struck with a hammer, they produce a melodic tone indicating a note of a musical scale. While the side of the hammer is wiped against the lip of the singing bowl, then the bowl sings in that similar musical frequency.

Hands-On Chakra Balancer

Hands-On Chakra Balancer is a complete traditional, practical energy-healing technique for balancing chakra. You can easily ensure it with your own hands unswervingly, or some inches above your body. At first, you snooze in a suitable place where you are not going to be bothered. Then you can pass some time belly-breathing and must take one or two minutes to center and ground. At the moment, you set a meaning for aligning as well as balancing your chakras. You can put one hand on the 1st chakra, and another hand on

2nd chakra. Then hold your hands at this point until you feel the energy align or until you begin to feel it pulse is in a patterned way or until you get any other sign such as just realizing that the 2 chakras are completely balanced. Don't feel bad if you don't find everything or anything or don't catch any other sign that the chakras will be balanced. Simply hold your hands on the 2 chakras for one minute or so, or until you find that it is the actual time to move on. Then, your aim to balance them will do the rest of the work. In the similar way, you move your hands to your 2nd and 3rd chakras and repeat the balancing. Similarly, move your hands to the 3rd and 4th and repeat the balancing. And so on. After you have balanced the last 2 chakras, take a little while to relish the sensation and feeling. Being conversant with the confirmation of having your chakras in balance will assist you recreate the state whenever you want to during the day. Must get up and must drink a glass of water. You can enjoy the rest of your day!

Working Procedure of Chakras For Improving Emotional and Spiritual Health and Support Aura

Chakra work is very much concerned when suitable in many of the sessions for physical, emotional and spiritual healing.

Auras Light Chakra Spirits are specially designed to assist open your chakras easily so that they can function actively. Overall health is sturdily influenced by chakra alignment and activity.

Additionally, when a chakra is completely awakened, it indicates that your awareness is adjusting to and integrating the spiritual facts related to that chakra.

Normal Chakra Activity Restoring

Everyone may have a question here. Why 12 chakras instead of 7 main chakras? There are actually 2 main types of concepts and configurations. The 12 chakras of the body are situated either both inside and outside or all inside:

1) Considering the first one, it locates 5 chakras outside along with the 7 primary chakras of the human body. This is actually the most common and general

way to characterize the 12-chakra system, with one chakra below the root chakra and the remaining ones above the crown.

2) Now, another one contains all 12 chakras inside, positioning 5 extra energy centers in-between the usually known 7 chakras.

These additional 5 chakras are located in different parts of the human body. 8th chakra located at the top and above the crown chakra of the chakras system. It is actually the highest point of the human body. The 9th chakra which is also known and recognized as the upper dan tien is located at Pineal Gland. 10th chakra is located above the heart chakra where it is also known as the spiritual chakra. 11th chakra is the pathwork to the soul. It is situated one and half inch above the belly button and the last 12th chakra is the source of power and strength. It is situated 8ich above the crown.

1st Chakra: Red

Better grounding, easier release of previous matters, better self-survival instincts, flow

2nd Chakra: Orange

Greater creativity and initiative, better relationships and emotional balance to keep calm and cool

3rd Chakra: Yellow

Better mental and emotional control over you and assist the digestive and nervous systems

4th Chakra: Green

Internal peace and synchronization with greater sympathy and expression of love; also a better overall stability

5th Chakra: Blue

Creativity and communication of ideas and thoughts

6th Chakra: Indigo

Better development of psychic capabilities, intuitive attunement, mystical growth & deeper and clearer understanding

7th Chakra: Violet

A sturdier link with intergalactic energy, greater spiritual consciousness, a closer personality with Oneness and a sense of contentment

8th Chakra: Magenta

Developing to our cosmic links outside Earth and assists open to channeling; produces a greater willingness to help in an unselfish way.

9th Chakra: Pink

Life creek purpose and meaning within Reality; dissolving of personal barriers and development of self-identity; helps greater attunement to Divine Love and respect

10th Chakra: Turquoise

Endorses mind/heart balance to better attain the Soul's resolve of "right expression"; assists lift unhappiness or negativity, and through profound harmony assists better utilize the services of nature.

11th Chakra: Gold

The dynamic "Yang" belief and the active forces of nature; carries knowledge that you have the skill to attain your life goal and sense of duty in accomplishing that purpose; aids move out of sluggish states; encourages greater consciousness of God as the doer of entire things and a sense of this present

12th Chakra: Silver

The inert instinctive "Yin" belief in creation and your deepest link with the Architect of the world and all of us - Divine spirit; with inaugural of this chakra you become more conscious of your Divine persistence, with the realization that entire things will be accomplished according to divine plan.

Chapter 4. Meditation Examples For 7 Major Chakras

Root Chakra Meditation

Sit in a comfortable place, cross-legged position. Then you must close your eyes and take a very deep breath. Once you are in a comfortable meditative state, focus on passing energy up throughout the bottom of your feet, and through your legs and also into the base of your spine wherever the root chakra is to be found. With each breath in; visualize the energy forming into a bright red ball of energy. With every single breath, the ball of energy becomes bigger and bigger and also starts to rotate in a clockwise direction. Carry on this until you surely feel the energy at the base of your spine. When you feel this and the root chakra is open, you will be set to move onto the Sacral Chakra.

Sacral Chakra Meditation

A sacral chakra meditation is the greatest way of opening this chakra. At first sit in a relaxed place and make your mind fully concentrates. Once you acquire into that meditative state, then you focus on the energy being fetched up through your feet as well as through your root chakra, then must up into your navel. Think a ball of orange energy making below your belly button which produces larger and larger with each deep breathe in. This orange ball of energy will begin to swirl in a clockwise position, then you will feel a small tingle in your lower abdomen as well as lower back where the sacral chakra is placed. Continue working on this till you actually feel the energy. It feels approximating a tingling or it could be a buzzing of energy flowing through you. Besides, you may or may not grow into sexually aroused, but either way is exactly fine. When you feel this one is open, you may go on to the Solar Plexus Chakra.

Solar Plexus Chakra Meditation

To meditate on this solar plexus, fetch energy up from the ground, then through your feet as well as legs. Besides, bring it up through your root, sacral chakras first, and then let it to reside in your upper abdomen, wherever the third chakra is positioned. Imagine a ball of yellow energy forming in this region, getting larger with each deep breathes. Focus on the energy rotating in a clockwise position as well as getting bigger and bigger until you feel the minor tingle in your upper abdomen. When you feel this Solar Plexus chakra is open, you can move onto the next Chakra.

Heart Chakra Meditation

Once you have gotten into that meditative state, turn on bringing energy up throughout your body hitting the root, sacral as well as solar plexus along the same way. With each breathe, this energy grows greater and courses in through your feet and up through your preceding chakras. Then imagine a ball of green energy starting in your chest area. This ball of energy will become larger and larger and swirl in a clockwise direction with every deep breathe in you take. Focus on beliefs of love and compassion yourself, as well as others. Once you feel the energy in your chest and also feel that your heart chakra is fully open, you may move to the next throat Chakra for knowing better.

Meditation of Throat Chakra

Once you are in a meditative state, and then focus on bringing energy up through your feet with each inhale. Flow the energy done each of your four previous chakras in addition to up to your throat. With every deep breath in; imagine a blue energy blooming around your throat rising bigger and bigger. Let your breath out all blocks and negativity from the throat and exchange them with effervescent blue energy. Then you can sense your throat muscles loosening up and may even gulp. This is faultlessly normal. When you feel your throat feels open and relaxed, you have completed this and move on to the Third Eye Chakra to know better.

Meditation of 3rd Eye Chakra

You reach into a relaxed meditative state; focus on energy coming up through your feet with every inhale. You may sure that bringing energy up through all of the five previous chakras, earlier focusing the energy on your third eye chakra in the midpoint of your forehead. With each gasp, imagine a purple ball of energy, increasing bigger and bigger where the third eye is situated. With each exhale, release any negativity or blocks that may be associated with your third eye. Continue this way until you feel a prickly sensation or warmth in the middle of your forehead. When this occurs, your third eye is at the present healed and opened and you may transfer on to the Crown Chakra.

Meditation of Crown Chakra

Take a long, deep breath. As you let your breath out, move consideration to the highest place of your head, then envisage a chakra with violet color. The shady violet light of the chakra brightens your mind as well as the other parts of the body. You feel the energy from your crown chakra attaching you to the sky on the top and to the earth below, and to all in between, so you turn into one with existence. When you are ready, you can open your eyes and rise.

Conclusion

The 7 chakras in our human body are the energy centers in which energy or power flows though. Blocked energies often lead to the sufferings of human. So, it's important to know each pros and cons of chakras to lead a happy life by letting energies flow freely.

Thank You Page

I want to personally thank you for reading my book. I hope you found information in this book useful and I would be very grateful if you could leave your honest review about this book. I certainly want to thank you in advance for doing this.

If you have the time, you can check my other books too.

www.ingramcontent.com/pod-product-compliance
Lightning Source LLC
LaVergne TN
LVHW021744060526
838200LV00052B/3467